TWO SHORT

SATAN
IS REAL

WENDY ERSKINE & STEPH VON REISWITZ

ROUGH TRADE BOOKS × MUSEUM OF WITCHCRAFT AND MAGIC

ENDOR

Furfur, I said, and the name echoed because no one was there. But earlier Furfur had been on top of the bus before springing to the shelter where he kicked down a load of rainwater that had gathered on the roof. The people walking past gazed up to see the mini cascade's origins. Furfur pressed the yellow bell for the length of the journey, the passengers getting irritated at the supposed malfunction. The driver had to keep stopping.

Furfur was so excited to get into the house, jumping up and down while I fumbled in my bag for the key. Once inside he hung warm and close to my leg like a cat. I liked it. Eventually he took a spot by the window and looked out. That first night Sam's mum Anita called round with a batch of scones she had baked. I thought you might like some, she said. They were on a tray covered in a tea towel. I knew that Furfur wouldn't want her around, so I kept her on the doorstep.

I'd invite you in but I have to go out soon, I lied.

Are you alright? she said.

Oh yeah fine.

You sure?

I'm fine. I'm great.

Well hopefully I'll see you soon, she said, and handed over the scones.

I closed the door.

Furfur was happy and the air in the living room turned a dancing golden. I was wrapped in a bandage of honeyed warmth.

Bandage of honeyed warmth? Yes, I know. But I'm trying to tell this as best I can because even now it is hard to understand it. All I can do is lay it out as it seemed. We had gone for a coffee that day, Anita and I, after visiting Endor. Anita left but I sat on and ordered another one. It was the café in the bookshop. The people at the next table were reading in an ostentatious fashion, holding up the covers so that everyone could see what they were. The woman, however she moved, hit herself in the face with her book. Startled, she rubbed her nose. I couldn't help laugh to myself. There was a pile of celebrity sports biographies constructed into a pyramid. They slapped onto the wooden floor as if pushed over. The next coffee arrived and I settled into my seat.

And then it was as if the air grew impatient in front of me. It seemed muscled. I looked at an empty table where, yes, there was the trace of something jumping on and off it with the energy of a child. On and off, on and off. Then, whatever it was hopped on to my knee, light and warm, before moving off and onto another table. It felt like Christmas when I was a kid and there was a new and complicated toy. This one wanted to go with me. Its outline, or the sense of it, was always changing. It was a deer up on its hind legs; a little girl in, what was it, knee socks; a lithe little pick-pocket, a monkey. Everyone around me was serenely unaware of this thing.

I thought, what a total acid trip.

And then the word came. Furfur. Furfur.

When I had gone to the house to be the bridesmaid it was clear that even the make-up artist knew. All the others got lavish eyes, whereas I had nothing more than a little taupe tight-line. The hairdresser was the same: just a low pony tail for me.

They whispered, so brave. Even the corks of the sparkling wine didn't pop with any extravagance. There was just an abortive little sound and then we all drank it as if it was tea. The dress, when I put it on, was far too big. There was so much fabric across my chest. Jacqui had said she'd understand it if I didn't want to come but I insisted. It was fine. I would be there. But as my hair was pulled into that low pony tail, I knew I should have stayed at home.

When I appeared in the church, as many people were looking at me as looking at Jacqui making her stately procession towards Jonesy in a dress that had cost almost two grand. They had seen the newspaper front pages and the updates online. I had been interviewed on the TV; they wanted to do it outside the house but it was windy and so our hair kept whipping across our faces, Anita and me. There were so many dopey rumours, that he had been drugged up, that he'd been doing crazy stuff with a prostitute, that he'd been depressed for ages and had finally decided to end it all.

You look lovely, Jacqui said. The make-up really suits you.

One night when we were out with our crowd Sam put his arm around me and I didn't resist. He was warm, solid and a person not prone to issues. That was it: a few meals, a few nights out, a few weekends away and we moved in together. Competent's pretty pejorative, I know. The dull diligence of it. But Sam was so competent at everything: any sport he tried, any exam he did. He could cook, could help a neighbour build an extension. He was always the same. No complications. So it was ridiculous that he could go missing.

The wedding photographer wore a tweed suit complete with waistcoat. He arranged everyone in various configurations and said to me on one occasion, Hey Smiler. I ignored it. But somebody must have had a word with him because he then stopped asking me to be in the photographs altogether.

It sounds mundane maybe, but in the early stages one of the remarkable things about Furfur was the way that he could tidy things up. It was quite amazing. The kitchen was transformed after Furfur had worked his magic. The noise he seemed to make while doing this was like the chase scene from a cartoon, a madcap play of glockenspiel sounds. In just a matter of seconds there was order and a kind of clean lemon smell. That's how it was, anyway, when Furfur first came.

Back then there was so much fun to be had. Furfur made sure that programmes I hadn't seen since being a kid could come on; there were times when the people in the programmes would slip out of the screen and into the room and then back again. The first time it happened it was a dopey rom-com where people were having brunch. My living room became the diner; I could smell the coffee and the waitress lifted the plates high as she negotiated the sofa and the little table. Sometimes, if the TV wasn't on, the contents of the room just moved like a kaleidoscope, glittering and absorbing. A slow blink and it would all disappear. It was wonderful, beautiful really. If I had a bath, the rainbow bubbles would be floating up and around the room, bursting with delicate little pops to reveal puffs of pastel powder. Colours glowed. I could stare at something like a mug for hours, marvelling at its perfect cylindrical form and the flower design that seemed to bloom.

It was entirely possible from my sofa to travel back in time with Furfur if I wanted to. I saw my legs clad in thick grey wool stockings and black boots when I went to the Great Exhibition. I tried out Laurel Canyon. It wasn't that you could see it exactly, but you could feel it, the atmosphere. I could always still see my own legs dangling off the sofa. But it was odd: when faced with the opportunity to go anywhere or see anything what I picked was sometimes clichéd. I went to Woodstock, saw the Stooges, went to the building of the Pyramids, Paris 1968, and to the ceremony where Hattie McDaniel won an Oscar. I watched Lenny Bruce on stage a couple of times. I watched Valerie Solanas shoot Andy Warhol. I went to my own 4th birthday party. I liked my parents in the memories from when I was a kid. They were always trying to phone me but I only contacted them back when I knew they were likely to be out. I left cheerful messages on their answerphones. People knocked on my door, including them no doubt, but I tended not to answer. Why would I, when I had all of this going on?

I thought that I wanted to see the most beautiful woman in the world but Helen of Troy looked kind of plain to me, her hair just hanging down limply and so I saw Kim Kardashian too and marvelled at her ass and the smoothness of her skin. I saw Claudia Cardinale and Monica Vitti, both beautiful too. At that time Furfur was all laughter. He loved to see my reaction to things, would jump up and down in delight.

But then—then Furfur started to get moody, teenage. It was hard to keep him happy. He would mope all day when I had to go to work. He wanted to be brought along and although I recognised that it was boring to be alone for hours, I didn't want him there. They had been so good about everything to do with Sam, I didn't want them to be inconvenienced by Furfur's possible antics. And then the house started to feel damp all the time. I had got into the way of wearing Sam's clothes, but when I put them on, they never felt dry. I started turning the heat up full, but it made no difference.

The hen night was in Mullingar, at a hotel that specially catered for hen nights. At the next table in the restaurant there had been a group with matching T-shirts: Big Muff, Cute Muff, Crazy Muff, Grumpy Muff. Crazy Muff got so drunk that when she fell off her chair, she pulled half the food from the table with her. Ours was a more sedate affair. We felt comparatively demure in our little pink headbands. Later the talk turned to men and with all of the petty jealousies and attempts at control I felt lucky that I had Sam. He'd only had one serious girlfriend before me. She was called Jodee. What in the hell type of name is that anyway? I'd said to him. They'd gone out right from when they were at school. She still texted him to say Happy Christmas. It annoyed me. Well good you can enjoy yourself now you've got the little message from the love of your life. Not really Christine, he'd reply. She'd been really sporty; she'd captained a women's football team and she had been a gymnast. The first time we had sex all I could think about as I lay there was that what had just happened must have been so fucking boring compared to gymnast Jodee who could contort herself into such intriguing and exciting positions. I imagined her at the end of the bed as though it was an Olympic beam. Every sex-worker or pole dancer that I envisaged in Amsterdam was in a leotard, was Jodee. Because that's where the stag night was the next weekend.

At lunchtime on the Sunday I got a call from Jacqui. She said that she didn't want to panic me or anything because most likely it was totally explainable, but no one had seen Sam since the night before. The rest of the guys now needed to go for the plane but he wasn't with them.

So when did they last see him?

About two in the morning, Jacqui said. After they'd been to wherever they'd been. They were going to try one more place and if they couldn't get in, then they were going back to the hotel. Jonesy says that he wasn't with them any more at that point.

Well don't panic, I said. Maybe he'll meet them at the airport or something. It's so not like Sam to miss a flight!

Should they contact the police do you think? Jacqui asked.

No, I said. What would be the point? I was imagining the hard time I was going to give him. Oh yeah well you are not Mr All That because do you remember the time you got so wasted in Amsterdam you missed the flight. You too can be a dick you know!

I phoned Sam but there was no answer. Again and again, no answer.

The day after, Anita, Jonesy and I flew to Amsterdam. The only time I was ever at the airport was for a holiday. It was always connected to a sense of expectancy. There were the things that I always did when I was there, like buy a couple of magazines and go for a coffee, contentedly look out at the planes. From Sam's big sweatshirt and his grey jogging bottoms that were way too big for me I could smell his warmth and that outdoors, buttery scent that was his. It was strange to know what to do. It didn't seem right to sit where we normally would have done to have a coffee. I phoned my parents to say that we couldn't find Sam. They wanted to come too, make the 80 mile journey to the airport but I said no. Because I still felt at that moment that he was just stuck somewhere—he'd bumped his head maybe, had gone to a party and maybe got sick. I could see him lying in a hospital bed somewhere, the relief and laughter when we came in and said, what are you like? Didn't you give us all such a scare?

On the plane Anita got a small bottle of wine and Jonesy got a beer.

You not having a drink Christine? Anita said. I am beside myself. This is hell on earth. And you don't want a drink?

No.

You could get a gin and tonic.

I don't want a drink, Anita.

Anita thought the Airbnb was costing a lot of money. Wouldn't you think, she said, that under the circumstances they would have reduced the price? I told them what happened. When I emailed the woman, I told her. But she didn't even mention it.

It's not their issue, I said.

It actually is their issue, Anita said. Their city is where he went missing.

We had to pick up his bags from the police station because they hadn't been taken from the hotel. Jonesy was going to do that, plus show the police exactly where they had been on that night, if he could remember. Anita and I had to meet a man and woman from the embassy and then we had hospitals and homeless shelters to visit. When we got out at Central Station Anita started to cry. The canal looked black and the canal houses with their sloping angles slouched. I knew Sam was dead then. I knew that we would not find him.

At the Airbnb the woman had left a key in the bookshop downstairs. There was nowhere comfortable to sit, only a couple of hard chairs. We ended up on the double bed with bags of crisps and a bottle of water from a shop on the corner. Jonesy was embarrassed and upset. Once he brought the bag back from the police station, he went out again for a drink. Anita took everything out of it, folded it up and then put it in again, took it out, folded it again, put it in again. I didn't tell her where I was going when I slipped out to one of the bars where Jonesy said they had been. It was quiet, with the tea lights flickering sadly. I had flyers in my bag but I knew there was no point showing them to the smiling girl in the stripy tights who brought over my drinks.

When we returned again, a week later, we stayed in a hotel in Nieuwezijds Voorburgwal. The police had contacted us. They'd found an Algerian guy who said that he had seen someone fall into a canal. It looked like he tripped. But when the guy peered into the water he couldn't see anything. He thought maybe he was mistaken. But then he had seen one of the flyers somewhere. The police had then searched the area where the Algerian guy said he was and they had found Sam.

Jonesy couldn't come because the wedding had happened and he and Jacqui were now on honeymoon in Mauritius. I felt sorry that their married life was getting off to this start. He kept phoning to ask how we were, and Jacqui kept sending messages. The police reckoned that Sam had been urinating by the canal and had lost his balance. This apparently happened to many men who drowned in Amsterdam. There was a thing called micturition syncope, the phenomenon of fainting during urination. Due to a combination of alcohol consumption and pissing while standing, the amount of blood going to the brain decreases as blood vessels expand. They knew it was him; they had already identified the body from dental records. I couldn't remember Sam ever going to the dentist. His teeth were as you would expect, really lovely. They showed us some CCTV footage of men's heads, bobbing down a crowded street. It was grainy and it was impossible to know which one was him.

Anita said, So that's the last we see of him?

We watched it again and again. I just don't know which is him, she said. I don't know which is him!

Sam could swim really well, she said. I took him swimming from when he was no size.

And then she started crying.

He was brought back home and the funeral took place in the same church as the wedding. Jacqui and Jonesy were there with tans. Everyone from the stag night was in attendance. There had been a story in the paper about how all the guys on the stag night had gone to the same primary school but one of them hadn't returned from Amsterdam. They'd used the photo of the P7 group with all the stag night participants circled.

I couldn't sleep in our bed. It felt massive. I dragged the duvet through to the sofa and fell asleep there. I woke up with the TV still blaring. As soon as I got in from work, I put on the immersion so that I was able to fill the bath up to the top and lie there, immobile, with the lights off. There was Sam everywhere in the flat. His bottles of sauces in the cupboard, his trainers under the bed. Around the sink there was the traces of when he had last had a shave. There was the eczema cream for the rash he got on his arms. I stuck my hands in the pockets of his clothes and got receipts for stuff, milk, bread and washing-up liquid in one place, a packet of socks and a black T-shirt somewhere else. A flyer from a street preacher. I wouldn't even take something like that. I'd walk straight past. He'd take it to be polite.

When Anita came round after the funeral she said, So you're back to work.

Well yeah Anita. I think it's best. I'm just trying to keep busy. And I need to pay the rent.

Oh, I couldn't even think about going back just yet.

Her eyes could hardly close because they were so swollen with weeping.

I've no one now, she said.

Well you've still got me, I said, although I wondered if that was much consolation.

I've been thinking, she said, and I don't know why we didn't say it to those people over there. If people just faint when they are having a pee, why aren't people keeling over in their own toilets. Never heard of it happening in all my years. Banging their heads on the ceramics? Never heard of it. Have you?

No, I said.

Anita said that there was a place in Belfast. A friend had told her about it. It was in one of the old buildings near the city hall. Scottish Providence. The friend said that when you walked in, it just had a special atmosphere. Not creepy or anything.

I know where it is, I said. The entrance is next to the chopped salad place.

It's called the Endor Centre, Anita said. The woman in charge used to run a yoga place in the States.

I made a face.

Yes well my friend, actually more of a friend of a friend, her mother dropped dead just out of the blue and they were so distressed and they were able to get in contact with her somehow via the people at this Endor Centre. You know, she didn't appear as a ghost, but she did appear some way or other.

Let me know how you get on, I said.

Oh come with me Christine. Please. Will you?

I half expected the woman down below in reception to snigger when we said we were going to the Endor Centre but she didn't. Instead she directed us to a waiting area on the second floor with dark painted walls and white tiling. There were a few interiors magazines on a coffee table and some brochures relating to injectable facial treatments, which Anita nervously read. A young guy appeared, called Anita's name, and led us to a room that looked out onto the city hall. I'd expected people round a table, a séance with a load of ectoplasm. Instead there was just one woman who asked us if we wanted a herbal tea.

The woman wore a slash neck, black dress that was expensively draped. Her bare legs were tanned and her eyes very blue. I thought they were probably contact lenses. Anita told her about what had happened to Sam. The woman turned to me, waiting for my contribution. I just looked back. There was music playing, a man and woman singing with some old harpsichord or something.

What's that? I asked.

Purcell, she said. Her accent sounded more Irish than American.

She began to talk about membranes, about semi and selectively permeable ones. It was reminiscent of the pseudo-science in ads for face creams, the peptides or collagen whatnots. But it wasn't swishy hair or glowing skin. It was transgressing boundaries of life and death.

The woman said that we would need to try to communicate with Sam in a formalised way. She said that this should happen just before daybreak and finish just after. We were to download an Endor app which would calculate for us the correct times according to the date and the location. Plus, the app would play appropriate sounds for the duration. She explained that we might think very little is happening—just occasional bubbles of sound—but that there was much going on undetectable to our ears, in the same way that there were frequencies which only young people could hear.

Or dogs, I said.

This was how it was to start. We would get a code to download the app for free and there would be a session the next week to discuss

what progress had been made. The woman produced a card reader and Anita got out her purse.

It's just, she said, that I can't believe he has gone. And what we were told. That he keeled over when he was going to the toilet.

But he hasn't gone, the woman said. Not really.

Before we left Anita said to the woman that she couldn't wait for the next morning. It was just so scientific the way the app calculated the right times.

When Anita phoned me the next morning to ask if I'd done the app, I said no.

Anita said that it had felt quite magical. But that the next time she would actually go outside. Into nature. I'm getting into the car, she said, and driving down to the football pitches, you know, at Alexandra Park Avenue. It will be really nice out in the open and I think I'll really feel him there. Don't forget to do it tomorrow, Christine!

I went back with her to Endor the next week, although I didn't feel like it. The woman wore another draped dress. Her hair was piled on her head in a messy bun and she had geometric earrings, little red triangles.

What's that music? I asked.

Handel, the woman said.

Anita was talking about how she had really felt so close to Sam this week. And the woman said that that was wonderful but there were ways that she could develop this, involving signing up for other sessions. She repeated the permeable and semi-permeable membrane speech. I looked around the room, and up at the fine cornicing of the ceiling. That must have been making me dizzy because it seemed as if the plasterwork was being extruded, and moving towards me. The smell of the woman's perfume was like ginger and smoke. It seemed to shake out of the folds in her dress when she moved her hands to illustrate this point or that. The old defunct fireplace was filled with logs. In amongst them I thought I saw antlers growing and branching.

Christine, Anita said, you'd agree with that, wouldn't you?

Sure, I said. Absolutely.

In front of the logs there was something brown: a tail unconnected to a body. It swished one way and then another. It was as if it had been drawn in the air with strokes of charcoal. I wondered if the woman saw it too because her eyes moved briefly in that direction before fixing again on me. I looked out the window at the solidity of the City Hall, white and square.

Then the woman's bun fell down. The clips must have come loose and next thing the elaborate mess hung around her shoulders. Even Anita laughed a little at that. The woman smoothed it as she continued to talk, but one hand kept reaching up to fiddle with an earring. Anita talked about how she was making progress with Sam. She was able to enter into a dialogue with him, as the woman said, with his answers just appearing in her mind like things re-surfacing from the bottom of a pond. He said he wished he'd never gone to Amsterdam, never gone. He said that he was looking forward to coming home and then because there was only one toilet in the little bar they were in, he went outside, and then he couldn't remember but he felt faint. He didn't hurt himself, didn't bang his head or anything but he was watching them every day and what they were up to. He had gone but maybe he hadn't really gone. The woman smiled. Anita said that just generally she had been feeling better about everything and that she had joined a walking group. The fresh air was good for her and she had made some friends. There was a woman there whose daughter took a drugs overdose many years ago and that they always find themselves falling into step beside each other, even though their kids aren't, weren't at all similar. And then after that was when we went for a coffee to the bookshop and Furfur first appeared. Back when Furfur was fun.

But it became hard to remember the playful Furfur. It seemed like an eternity before. Even the sulky teenager had been totally eclipsed. One time I found myself with Furfur on eBay buying lots of clothes: prairie dresses in sprigged prints and white broderie anglaise skirts that brushed the ground, blouses that fastened with big bows, shirts with lace collars. They arrived in padded envelopes from all over the world. Everything was shapeless, voluminous and Furfur was pleased when I put them on. The scissors in the kitchen were shiny and the points when I looked at them seemed to twitch. It made sense to cut my hair which had started to feel thick and weighty. I cut it really short around my ears, leaving a long lock at each side. Then I chopped at the back of it.

In work they said, Wow Christine. That new cut is something else. I mean the clothes, they were different but the hair too! You are really embracing a new look.

But the boss called me in about the food. Christine, he said, I don't know what's going on but that is just not healthy to be eating that kind of thing. We are worried about you.

What I wanted to eat were cubes of stewing steak, raw. I found it satisfying, chewing them. I loved the different textures of the fat and the meat. I brought them in a lunch box and to eat afterwards a packet of fizzy chewy coke bottles. I would eat one after the other at the computer. My screensaver at work was Sam and then it suddenly wasn't. It was something that looked like that thing that turkeys have, a wattle, blotchy, hanging skin. What in the name of god is that? somebody asked. It's art, I said. From a gallery. I changed it back to Sam but it went back to the wattle again.

I remember saying that I didn't think the raw meat was so different to sushi.

Christine, believe me, it's different, the boss said. You need to take time off. Seriously. We've appreciated you trying to keep on going after what happened. His voice trailed off. But yeah, we want you to take time off.

I didn't argue. I hadn't been feeling so well. I got headaches within ten minutes of getting up and there was always a taste in my mouth that I couldn't get rid of at all. I'd clean my teeth but it wouldn't matter. I started brushing them with the kitchen disinfectant squirter, the apple scented thing, and although it stung at times and was harsh if swallowed, it did help a bit. My skin had got to be always itchy. I tried to find some of Sam's old creams but they were gone, dumped with the rest of his stuff in a skip a street away.

I saw Jacqui in the street one day before I stopped going out. She came up and hugged me.

Christine! she said. She looked scared.

I've tried to call round to see you. Have you not got any of my messages?

Furfur, who used to jump on and off tables, used to fizz with energy, had grown kind of sluggish and fat. The light had started to bother him and I covered the windows with newspapers so that the house could be in a state of perpetual twilight. I liked to hear Furfur's breathing, which would fill the whole place, a slow inhalation and exhalation. It calmed me. At night Furfur surrounded me inside and out. I felt held. But I couldn't move. It was like cloud with muscle. I could get panicked if I thought about it, if I thought, I want to move my arm, but if I accepted it, it was nice.

Sometimes people banged on the door. It was most likely Anita or my parents. They went away eventually. There were bruises on my skin from injuries that I couldn't ever remember getting. I could stare at the filament in the one light bulb that still worked for an infinity.

One morning I woke up to sounds that I hadn't heard before. A metallic tink from the pipes. And beyond that a rush of white noise fissle. I half tried to work out what it was. After lying there for some time I realised that it was water running. When I put my feet to the ground, the floor of my bedroom was wet. In the bathroom, both taps gushed water, overflowing the basin. The bath too was flooding the room, a sheet of water pouring over the edge, and in the kitchen the roar was almost overwhelming. A remote thought surfaced about how we always used to complain about our water pressure, our paltry trickle of a no power shower. There was an oily, sour smell from the water and things floating in it, webbed stuff like wet wipes. Furfur came storming down and he was angry. What had I done? I hadn't done anything! The water was getting darker now, ink black. When I lifted my foot, I thought it would be stained dark. The house was freezing cold.

Furfur started banging on the windows. They were vibrating in their frames, pulsing. Furfur was trying to fill the kitchen, stretching out so that he spanned worktops and the cooker, went underneath the water on the floor. Something was behind me and when I turned around Sam was stood there, dripping water. His face was puffed and his eyes didn't close. He opened his mouth as if to speak but all that came out was black wetness. When he looked at me, I felt the bruises on my skin ache and I put my hand up to touch my face which felt crusted with scabs. Furfur's

muscle rippled and flexed, rippled and flexed. Furfur wanted me
to think of things he had shown me, thrown up on the wall night
after night, red depravity. The bodies of the villagers. The soldiers
with their bamboo. Faces in agony. A golden heel on a tanned and
lithe foot a beautiful rich foot grinding on a little hand so that
the skin eventually broke and then with a sickening crush the
heel negotiated tendon and bone. Arms hacked off. There was the
hospital photo of a child with a prolapsed gut after a sexual assault.

What to shore up against this? Sam stared at me, waiting. Furfur
had brought friends and they were slithering over the kitchen
table, stretching their mouths open like cats. They danced across
the water. But all I could think of was Jesus, the way he was in
the pictures: holding a lamp by the door, on the cross, in the white
robes and holding his hands up to heaven. Furfur laughed. Ha
Ha Ha. It rang round the kitchen and was inside me. It was only
art, only pictures. And then into my mind came of all things
Anita. Anita with her scones, always too dry anyway, but Anita
with her scones knocking on my door, Anita canteen assistant
for thirty years in the same school, slipping some kids extra food,
Anita whose husband had left her when Sam was one, Anita
never slagging him, Anita minding her ex and his new partner's
kids when the new partner was in hospital with breast cancer,
Anita folding her dead son's clothes with love, Anita with that
stupid little sign in her bathroom saying Anita diminutive of
Anna, from Hebrew Hannah, meaning gracious or favoured,
Anita who lined her sister's grave with moss so she would not
feel the cold, Anita who—

A seeming eternity to get to the hall. Just try, just try, just try.

The water ran out into the street and over Anita's shoes.
The bottoms of her jeans turned black.

What on earth? she said.

It was a fight to get back to the kitchen as the house pounded, Furfur's creatures scuttling through our hair, clawing. When Anita saw Sam standing there by the cooker she started to sob.

Son, she said. Son.

He held out his hands and we took them, the three of us a little triangle.

Furfur spoke out loud for the first time in a language we didn't understand, low and guttural. Ugly and loud.

We still held hands, our little triangle.

Furfur spoke again his babble.

We still held hands.

The taps still drip drip dripped but the rush was gone.

We still had our hands out, Anita and I, but Sam wasn't there anymore.

Sad, shy, Anita folded her arms. So, she eventually said. Let's get something dabbed on that face. You got any towels to mop up all of this water?

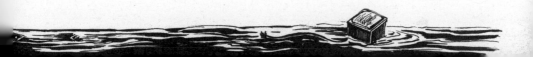

BRYGHT GEHENNA

In the charity shop windows on the road there's an assortment of goods: a child's wetsuit say, a Belleek vase, a pair of stripper shoes, a fibre optic light. There are two, sometimes three mannequins, always female. Someone who's made a donation might see their own clothes on the model in the window: their jacket certainly, the same little stain on the sleeve, but the arm at an unfamiliarly jaunty angle, the model smiling in a way they might not.

Inside the shops have started colour-coding the clothes, so that the rails run through the shades of the prism. The tangle of necklaces on display might be draped on a plastic hand. Shoes, bought for a wedding or court appearance and discarded afterwards, still look stiff. There will be a cardboard box of CDs, some still bearing the price labels from long defunct record shops. On occasion there will even be LPs. There may well be a treasure to be discovered by a collector but more likely on offer are pop compilations and light classical. There may well be country and western records, American certainly, but also albums featuring artists from Belfast or Armagh or Tyrone. Some of these will fall into the sub-category of country gospel. A person going through a record box in a charity shop might just come across the recordings of The Devine Family.

They might see the album with Pastor Ronnie James Devine, his wife and his son in a fishing boat. The sky looks ominous and the water choppy, but Pastor Devine's expression is stoical, as is his wife Dorcas's. Eleven year old Jamie's countenance is more difficult to determine. On the Christmas record, released some eight months later, they are in a room with an unadorned tree and a burning log fire. Dorcas Devine is at the table and Pastor Devine stands in front of the fire, one hand on the mantelpiece. Jamie Devine is sitting cross-legged on the floor, apparently reading a book. They might find the *Praise* album which features a highly tinted mountain scene of the type found on holiday postcards.

The records, if they are to be found, are almost forty years old, perhaps scratched, warped. The production sounds thin, the songs dated and rather Old Testament. The undoubted sincerity is perhaps a little embarrassing and the pedal-steel, often too loud, is intrusive. The trilling harmonies of Jamie and his mother are shrill.

Ronnie James Devine has a rich baritone voice. During a short-lived religious phase, Ernie McCormack, the boss of a little Belfast record label, found himself in the pastor's church one Thursday night and, although he got little from the sermon, was struck by the power of the singing emanating from the pulpit. Ernie McCormack had a roster of Irish traditional artists, plus a female country and western singer and her band. He saw a certain commercial potential in the dour figure at the front. The pastor wasn't sure whether entering into a venture with this man was in fact God's purpose, but he said that after prayer and reflection he came to the conclusion that he could do useful witness through it. The first record of the pastor's rendition of familiar old hymns was well received. It got airplay on the local Sunday night religious programmes and the pastor performed at any churches requesting his presence.

When it came to Ernie McCormack's attention that both Dorcas and Jamie Devine could hold a tune he decided that they should also appear on the records. The Devine Family: a good gimmick. People would like Dorcas, they would take to her. She was pretty in her own way. And all the old people would love the boy.

The Devine Family started to appear on local television. Jamie's hair was always trimmed for this, the newspaper put down on the kitchen floor, and he could see his mother's hand shake as she cut his fringe. The prospect of appearing on television frightened her. There would usually be some kind of rehearsal, even for live shows. When someone yelled cut, Dorcas's hand went to her temple. She always thought it was her fault. If Ernie McCormack was around the studio, he would pretend to cuff Jamie on the ear and then he would give him a pound note. Don't be spending it all in the one shop! he said every single time.

They were occasionally asked onto variety shows. Other familiar faces included the accordion band made up of four generations of the same family and twin magicians. The two youngest members of the accordion band were just a little older than Jamie but had no interest in talking to him. They pointed and whispered to each other: would you look at the goody goody wee cocksucker!

It was the final few months of primary school when he first started singing on the records. In his small school there was delight that one of their own should be elevated in such a way. He was required to sing in school assemblies and everyone asked him about being on the telly. When Jamie moved to secondary school however, there was a different attitude. On the first day someone in his new class said, here, you're not that wee fruit that does the singing?

That was the beginning. The school day was long. In the corridors between classes Jamie got used to people pushing him and shouting. Give us a song! Oi you, Holy Joe, what's up with you? Some joker started a way of having fun that was promptly taken up by everyone else in the school. It was called I saw wee Jamie Devine. I saw wee Jamie Devine downing ten cans of Kestrel then having a wank in his front garden. Well I saw wee Jamie Devine shagging his ma in Gresham Street while he was eating a burger. Well know what, I saw wee Jamie Devine sucking Bobby Sands's dick while he was singing 'Jesus Loves Me'. And so on. Before long there was no one in the school who did not know who wee Jamie Devine was.

People knew who Dorcas was too. Jamie heard them make comments when they were out. Paler than she looks on the telly. They must be rolling in it with those records, so do you not think she could get a better rigout than that? Shabby, to be honest. But they're against fashion or something, those religious sort of people. Would you fancy your man, big Ronnie? Would you? Don't think she actually does too much anyway. Just sort of sings along now and again. Money for old rope. And then the delayed peal of laughter as she and Jamie exited a shop.

When the Christmas album came out, it even had a television advert involving a montage of burning candles, a manger and Pastor Devine singing in a forest. There had been a flurry of snow one morning and they had taken the opportunity to go to a forest park for some impromptu filming. The actual album cover had taken a while to shoot. The log fire had sparked and sputtered, at one time sending out a spark that singed the pastor's trousers. Dorcas hadn't been well. She had been vomiting in the toilets and although she rarely wore any make-up, the photographer's assistant had to apply some because she was so pale. Smile Jamie, the photographer had said. Come on smile. It's Christmas. Look up and smile.

Although everyone wore the same school uniform the differences were significant. Mods had tight trousers and thin ties, a flash of white sock between trouser and shoe. The few skinheads wore their ties the same way but shortened their trousers so that a few inches of boot could be seen. The crowd into heavy metal had tight trousers but their ties had fat knots.

The form teacher brought in an old cassette player and allowed members of Jamie's class to bring in tapes to be played during lunch. Jamie sat eating his sandwiches with a couple of quiet boys who were Christians. Their ties were neither thin nor fat, but both wore a pin-badge to show they were members of the Scripture Union. The rule in the form room was that no one could play more than one side of a tape before it was someone else's turn, so the music ricocheted between mod and heavy metal.

There was a lot of concern about Satan at the time. It was said that many of the groups the young people were listening to were made up of devil-worshippers who took part in animal and even human sacrifice. In certain records, back-tracking concealed subliminal satanic messages. A look at the hellish images on the album covers suggested that much of this music was of a depraved kind. In school the pupils had plenty to say about what was meant to be going on. On any elevated ground, black masses were taking place. If you went up the Cavehill, for example, and saw the remains of a fire, that could only have been the result of a dark activity. People were breaking in to the local churches in the dead of night and conducting satanic rituals on the altars. Cats were disappearing, dogs were disappearing. Had people not heard about the farmer out near Ballyclare? He had found three cows dead, bizarre symbols carved in to their sides. Stay up until midnight and stare into the mirror and say the Lord's Prayer backwards and you would see the devil.

The local papers ran stories on the spread of satanic practices and churches warned young people not to get involved. Satan, despite what some might say, was very real. One of the boys in Jamie's class said that at the church his auntie went to they hired a cement mixer and asked all of the young people who liked heavy metal music to turn away from it. They were told to bring all of their records and badges to waste-ground at the back of the church hall. The minister read some Bible verses and they threw all of their stuff into a hole someone had dug and then the cement was tipped on top of it. But the cement didn't set for ages. It was really weird. It was as though the devil stuff wouldn't let the cement set. It was pure freaky.

Because of the relative infrequency of bands including the city on their tours, those who did come, such as AC/DC in 1979, or Siouxsie and the Banshees in 1980, were guaranteed a rapturous welcome. When tickets were released for the Bryght Gehenna concert, due to take place at the Ulster Hall on 15th April 1981, there was in some quarters delight. This group from Wolverhampton had been one of the stars at Castle Donnington Monsters of Rock the year before, and their bass player Gibby Crawford was from Belfast. Their album featured a hooded semi-naked woman in front of a scaffold. Their songs were both leaden and histrionic. The guitarist had inverted crosses tattooed on his arms and the singer, Denis Faccenda, had spent an indeterminate period on hallucinogens in Bolivia. The music at some of their concerts was so loud that people's ears seeped blood. Jamie listened to all this talk. The boys in his class were too young to get into the venue but everyone knew someone with tickets. The posters around the town displayed Bryght Gehenna in Germanic script against a fluorescent yellow background.

There are still street-preachers and singers in Belfast, as there were then. Better to appear before a congregation who gave undivided attention, not shoppers passing through, laden with poly bags. The Lord's word required concentration and it was sad to see tracts handed out in the street trampled underfoot. It would have taken an exceptional circumstance for the pastor to take to the streets but the Bryght Gehenna concert proved to be exactly that. There were people who felt compelled to make a stand against everything that this group represented. Bryght Gehenna. The biblical reference to the destination of the wicked, Gehenna the Lake of Fire, was not lost on the pastor. Jamie heard him ask Ernie McCormack if he had heard about Bryght Gehenna when they were driving along one evening to a performance at a faith mission. He had. Well, said the pastor, it's all very worrying. Don't think I've ever heard the like. And they're performing in the Ulster Hall. Ernie McCormack sighed. It's not satanic, Ronnie. It's just showbiz. That's just the way it is. Just the way it is. Showbiz. The pastor said nothing. Jamie saw a sign that said the place they were going to was still fourteen miles away.

On the evening of the protest, everyone was invited to gather outside the venue from 7.30pm onwards. Dorcas Devine wasn't well and couldn't go. The pastor stopped on the way to pick up some others whose placard bearing a Bible verse needed to be put into the boot. Two women bundled into the back and the one beside Jamie was his old Sunday school teacher. Even through her thick, decent coat he could feel her excitement. I'm quite fearful of what I might see, the other woman said.

On the way round to the Ulster Hall they encountered first a husband and wife from another church who were there for the same purpose, and then, as they got nearer, some others from their own. It was a cold, bright night. The windows of a bar they passed glowed amber and when the door opened as a crowd left, there was a swipe of laughter, the smell of cigarette smoke.

The long queue snaked around the side of the hall. Other protestors became visible as they drew closer; they stood in a rough semi-circle at the side of the entrance. Some held Bibles, and there was a little, wan singing. Oh Pastor Devine, a man said, rushing forward. Did you ever see such a crowd? Who would have thought there would have been so many of them! And indeed there were so many of them, the queue four or five people in denim and leather wide. One man at the front of the queue, his jeans didn't have a zip, but rather a criss-cross lacing arrangement, as though some mighty beast needed to be kept strapped down. One teenage guy kept coming up and doing strange signs with his hands. Jamie was standing next to the other woman who'd been in the back of the car; she stared ahead, mouthing the words of the hymn his father was singing as though she didn't see the sea of Bryght Gehenna fans in front of her.

Somebody started the chant. Terra! terra! terra! The stamping of feet and their arms in the air. Terra! terra! terra! descend. Terra! Terror! Tear her! Jamie had heard these words before, usually accompanied by people banging the desks with their fists. He knew most of the songs on the album, but the one he liked the best was 'Slave of Naamah': it began so quietly, just the guy singing, but then built up to pure noise. They would sing it tonight. What it would be to be in the crowd! It was the song that Bryght Gehenna often finished with, the final three minutes a slab of sound. Suddenly a girl appeared from out of the queue, right in front of where they were standing. What's that say? she said, pointing at a placard being held by one of the group. Can't read it. What's it say? Sub something? Sub what? Submarine?

The woman beside Jamie shouted out, Submit yourselves therefore to God. Resist the devil and he will flee from you.

Och aye, the girl said. Sure thing.

Hey big man! she shouted over at the pastor. Big man! Hey you!

And she pulled up her T-shirt to reveal large breasts which she jiggled, laughing. She turned around to face the cheers of the crowd. Cop a look at that then! she said. Hey big man!

The protestors gasped, appalled. Everyone stopped singing except for the pastor who continued without a beat. The sight had frightened some of them. When the doors opened into the foyer of the hall, the protestors stood until the last of the crowd had crossed the threshold. On the journey back home no one mentioned the incident with the girl. The old Sunday school teacher asked Jamie about how he got to school in the mornings. He said that quite often he walked but he did get the bus if it was raining. There were two different buses he could get, the school bus or the service bus.

There was a lot of discussion about the concert the next day in school. It had been recorded as the loudest concert in Northern Ireland ever. There had been a fight and somebody had been stabbed. The bass player had had sex with a girl that somebody or other actually knew. The Ulster Hall had been wrecked, thousands of pounds worth of damage, and there was blood down the walls in the toilet. Bands weren't going to be allowed to play there ever again. Well, one of the mods said, why not ask wee Jamie Devine about what happened because he was the one who was actually there.

Serious, wee Jamie was there?

Yeah. Somebody in one of the other classes was saying.

Were they trying to like, you know, sacrifice him?

Sacrifice Jamie Devine. If only. Now that I would pay to see.

And so the story unspooled about how Jamie Devine and his full on psycho da had been seen there by someone's brother and they were protesting against Bryght Gehenna. He was there with a bunch of old women all shaking signs and reading the Bible. The old women were screaming and shouting. Then the wee doll flashed her tits. The one time in my entire life, a boy said, that I've actually been jealous of Jamie Devine. Right in front of him, lucky bastard.

Don't know about that, somebody else piped up. I heard about that too and they said she was a boot. Was she a boot Jamie, or was she not?

The Devine Family had a release pencilled in for the summer. They had some new songs that had been written by an acquaintance of Ernie McCormack, still gospel songs but lighter, more upbeat, more suited to the better weather. It had been decided that the album cover should be taken at White Rocks, a beach near Portrush. But on the day when the photos were meant to be taken, Ernie McCormack, arriving to drive up to the coast with them, found them not ready to go. Dorcas Devine had locked herself in the bathroom. Make her a cup of tea, Ernie said. Jamie, can you make your mother a cup of tea? But Jamie, he said, you're not even changed yet! That's not what you're meant to wear. Where's the shorts and that wee casual jacket?

The pastor said, Get changed Jamie. Get changed now. Then the pastor went upstairs and banged on the door of the bathroom. Dorcas, he said. Ernie's here.

Well look, Ernie said, we can call it off. I can get a message to the photographer. It's dulling down anyway. Might be sensible to wait for a better day.

No, the pastor said. We'll be ready soon.

Jamie appeared in the outfit he had been given. He stood in the doorway. Ernie saw the long, thin legs, the shins shaded with hair. He saw that the fly was only half up because the shorts were so tight. The jacket ended two inches from his wrists.

Not too sure about that actually Jamie, Ernie said.

His hair was combed severely to one side, too far over, a mockery of a parting.

This is what I was told to put on, Jamie said.

Ernie looked at Jamie's face, the gaunt cheeks, the rash of spots on his forehead. His hair seemed darker. Actually, Ernie said, I'm thinking maybe we should just leave it for today. Your mum's not well.

The pastor came downstairs. Dorcas is just getting her things on, he said. She'll be down in a minute. Jamie, you're ready to go. That's good.

But by the time they got up to the coast the wind was whipping the rain against the windscreen. Nobody not even the pastor wanted to get out of the car.

In school, Jamie sat by himself at the desk in front of the teacher staring at the board's half-rubbed out hieroglyphs. The two boys he used to eat his lunch with sat behind him but he didn't turn around. When they started going to a new youth fellowship they had invited Jamie along. He asked them what they did there, and when they told him the scripture-based activities, he gave a laugh and said no thanks. One lunchtime the teacher noticed that her cassette player wasn't there.

Where'd you move it to, miss? one of the boys said.

I didn't touch it, she said.

Gonna be a rubbish lunch if we've got nothing to listen to!

Somebody'll have borrowed it. Probably it's been one of the other teachers. They'll bring it back tomorrow I'm sure.

The talk in the classroom turned back to the Twelfth in a couple of weeks' time: some boys had been involved in getting the materials together, taking orders from the overlords about what needed to be placed where. They discussed the best construction of palettes and tyres for optimum fire. They talked about the flags to be burnt, the various effigies of people who were hated.

Jamie had started with dice. He got the bus into town and went to Woolworths where he walked up and down the aisles, feigning an interest in this and that, a couple of pounds from Dorcas's handbag in his pocket. He bought some sweets from the Pick 'n' Mix, smiling at the woman when she handed him back the change. She looked as if she half-recognised him. There was an aisle with notebooks and writing pads, notelet sets, pens, pencils, rubbers. Some rubbers were shaped like strawberries, others were in the shape of cartoon lions and elephants. There were rubbers that were also dice. He slipped one into his pocket, felt a thrill. Then he took another, and another. The cassette player was less enjoyable because it was bigger. He came in to school early when the classroom was still empty, put it in a plastic bag and transferred it in his locker. He waited after school until everybody had gone before he headed home.

He could have stolen the tape from someone's bag in school but he didn't want to do that. In the phone book he looked up the addresses of record shops in the town, but the first one he went to didn't have what he was looking for. In fact it had hardly any tapes at all. He would have preferred a record—the cover!—but if he wanted to play it in his room he would have had to steal a record player. In the first shop the records were catalogued by genre. There were various different sections including a gospel one, and if he had looked there he would probably have seen himself. But Jamie found what he was looking for in another shop, where the man at the till was too deep in conversation with his two friends who leaned across the counter to notice Jamie reaching up for the cassette and slipping it in to his inside pocket. He could have slipped in half the shop without the man noticing.

It didn't work, staring in the mirror at midnight, reciting the Lord's Prayer backwards, even when it was written out on a sheet in front of him. He didn't see even the outline of the devil in the bathroom mirror, just his own face, disappointed and slightly relieved. Jamie turned around to see Dorcas at the bathroom door in her dressing gown.

NEMA. REVE DNA REVE ROF
YROLG EHT DNA
REWOP EHT DNA MODGNIK
EHT SI ENIHT ROF
LIVE MORF SU REVILED
TUB NOITATPMET OTNI
TON SU DAEL DNA
SU TSNIAGA SSAPSERT
OHW ESOHT EVIGROF
EW SA, SESSAPSERT RUO
SU EVIGROF DNA DAERB
YLIAD RUO YAD SIHT
SU EVIG. NEVAEH NI

I was just getting a drink of water, she said.

I'm just going to clean my teeth, he replied.

From the bedroom there was the noise of the pastor's snores.

Jamie slept at the top of the house. His room had a desk, a bed and a wardrobe. Dorcas came in twice a week to collect his washing and hoover but other than that it was left undisturbed. A ritual began. When the pastor and Dorcas were asleep, Jamie got a bag of flour and marked out a small circle with it on his wooden floor. Then he put his things in the centre. The dice he would roll until they were sixes and he would place them so they made a triangle. He would have taken something from the church but it was plain: no ornaments, no crosses or goblets or things like that. The only thing he could get was an arrangement of dried flowers in an old jar. He broke off their heads and crushed them to dust. This was sprinkled at the edge of the circle. He had drawn a pentangle on a broken compact mirror of Dorcas's. That too was put in the circle. Jamie put on the tape of Bryght Gehenna. It demanded to be played loud, but he couldn't risk turning up the dial beyond three, four at the most. And then he took his place in the middle of the circle. He would wait until the second or third song before pulling down his pyjama bottoms.

Sometimes the woman from the Pick 'n' Mix would present herself, or a pretty girl from the accordion band, but he would bat them away to think instead of the one from the concert who had bared her breasts. He could see them vividly, appalling and moonlike. He thought at other times of Denis Faccenda from Bryght Gehenna.

There were other Bryght Gehenna tapes Jamie wanted to listen to. He'd heard them talking about them in school. Live recordings. He went back in to the town,
to the same shop where before it had all been so easy. He scanned the cassette boxes, looking for the familiar jagged typeface, and there it was.
He put it in the palm of his hand.

Hey! came a shout.

Jamie turned around.

Jamie!

It was Ernie McCormack, coming out of the back of the shop. Next week, Jim, he shouted to the other man.

So, Jamie, what you up to? This where you're hanging around this weather?

Jamie shrugged. He felt the tape in his pocket.

You got a spare twenty minutes or so? Ernie asked. Because if you do, I got a load of stuff ready for posting I could do with a hand with.

Ernie's pokey second floor office was only a couple of minutes' walk away. There was an old typewriter at a table, but mostly it was just cardboard boxes, some empty, some full of records. There were posters on the walls for groups that Jamie had never heard of, a line of tickets dating back to the '70s.

Move those boxes there off that chair Jamie, Ernie said. Give yourself a bit of room.

The cardboard gave way when Jamie lifted it and he only managed to hold onto a few albums as they fell onto the floor.

Ernie sighed. Hard to shift, that stuff. Country singer-songwriter. But then everything seems hard to shift these days.

He gave Jamie a list of addresses that needed to be put on other boxes, once they'd been assembled from their flat state. There was a leaning pile of Devine Family albums under the table. Jamie could see the one with him sitting on the floor pretending to read a book.

How's your mum? Ernie asked.

Fine.

You rehearsing any new songs?

No, Jamie said. Weeks ago they had tried but the parts had to be switched because he couldn't reach the high notes anymore.

Ernie lifted a record with a cover of two women in white dresses sitting on a wagon. He looked at it then put it down, before reaching into his inside pocket for his cigarettes. A match rasped as it caught light. They'll hopefully do well, he said, taking a long, first draw. Although you never know.

He pointed to the boxes, the records piled up against the wall, the bulldog-clipped invoices and bills that sat beside the typewriter. Hard to know which way the wind is going to blow, he said.

Yeah, agreed Jamie.

So, Ernie said, the Devine Family. He paused. End of the road really for the Devine Family. You know what I mean. You understand what I mean. Maybe your daddy can continue, maybe there's a market for it, small enough but a market. The three of you though...

Jamie kept on folding a box.

End of the road, he said.

You got any sellotape? For these boxes?

Listen though. Listen to this. When you look back, you can be proud of what you've done. Even if people think it's shit. Even if a lot of people think it's shit. He reached for a Devine Family record. Because this stuff, this thing, exists longer than you. When you're gone it'll still be here. I'm under no illusions, we ain't producing the Sistine Chapel here. But something of some kind has been created. It's been created.

Sure, Jamie said. When he finished boxing up the records, Ernie gave him a five pound note but he didn't say don't spend it all in one shop. He shook Jamie's hand. The windows in the town were full of white clothes and coconuts and fake cocktails. Summer was coming even if it was raining. In the arcade he went into the sweet shop to get a box of matches. Although Jamie was half expecting it, the old guy who served him didn't query what he wanted them for. The café in Woolworths was still open, so he would put in some time there until he got his bus. He could get an orange juice from that tank where the fake oranges bobbed, churned around by the paddles.

It was the end of the day and they had already started to put some of the chairs on top of the tables. Jamie took a seat in a booth at the back. The woman at the till had her back to him and the only other people at a table were two old women wearing hats. He took a sip of orange and got the matches from his pocket. He lit one and held it against the plastic seat. Nothing happened initially, but then it started to bubble. Next the chemical smell and the plastic turning dirty brown. He shook out the match, then lit another one, did the whole thing again. He took a sip of orange. McCormack was wrong. To destroy was the real thrill. The seat was left scarred in six neat lines. He had tried to bring the flame as close as he could to the side of his hand before the pain became too much.

Where have you been? Dorcas said when he got back.
I was worried.

Just went into town. Got the bus.

Tea'll be ready in half an hour.

Sure.

Jamie?

Yeah?

Half an hour or so. Her hand hovered at her temple.

He waited that night until he knew that they were asleep to go downstairs to where the candles were kept in case of a power cut. In his room he drew out his flour circle and arranged the candles in the shape of a pentangle. Their glow was beautiful when they were lit. Could you be thrilled and totally calm at the same time? Yeah, he thought so. He sprinkled the dead flowers, what remained of them. He sighed, thinking of Bryght Gehenna. McCormack was right really when he said they were showbiz. On that one point he was right. He wanted silence for what he was going to do, didn't need any distraction. To destroy was what was required. That seat, he had left it in some state. The matches in his hand demanded more than thin candles; he wanted to watch things distorting and buckling, clean flames consume and destroy.
It was hard to know where to start.

WENDY ERSKINE

WENDY ERSKINE WORKS IN BELFAST. HER SHORT STORY COLLECTION 'SWEET HOME' WAS PUBLISHED BY THE STINGING FLY PRESS IN 2018 AND PICADOR IN 2019. IT WAS SHORTLISTED FOR THE REPUBLIC OF CONSCIOUSNESS PRIZE AND THE EDGE HILL PRIZE, AND LONGLISTED FOR THE GORDON BURN PRIZE. HER WRITING HAS APPEARED IN ANTHOLOGIES BY DOIRE, DOSTOYEVSKY WANNABE, FABER & FABER, NEW ISLAND, NO ALIBIS, REPEATER, THE STINGING FLY, WINTER PAPERS, AND IN VARIOUS JOURNALS. HER WORK HAS BEEN BROADCAST ON BBC RADIO 4 AND RTE RADIO 1.

I

I

STEPHANIE IS AN ARTIST AND ILLUSTRATOR WITH A PENCHANT FOR THE MYSTERIOUS AND THE DARKLY FUNNY. HER WORK INCLUDES PICTURES, COMICS, MURALS, ANIMATION, AND INSTALLATIONS. AS A CORE MEMBER OF LONDON ART COLLECTIVE LE GUN, AS WELL AS INDEPENDENTLY, SHE HAS WIDELY EXHIBITED IN THE UK, EUROPE, THE US, JAPAN, AND CHINA. HER FIRST BOOK OF MURDER MYSTERIES 'MURDER MOST PUZZLING' (CHRONICLE BOOKS) IS PUBLISHED IN AUGUST 2020. SHE LIVES AND WORKS IN LONDON.

STEPH VON REISWITZ

II

ENDOR

WHEN CHRISTINE'S BOYFRIEND GOES MISSING
IN AMSTERDAM, SHE TRIES TO FIND OUT WHAT
HAPPENED TO HIM, EVENTUALLY RESORTING TO
THE ENDOR CENTRE IN BELFAST CITY CENTRE.
BEFORE LONG, HOWEVER, CHRISTINE FINDS
THAT SHE HAS UNLEASHED A NEW, POWERFUL,
UNCONTROLLABLE LOVER.

BRYGHT GEHENNA

JAMIE IS A MEMBER OF A COUNTRY GOSPEL ACT,
THE DEVINE FAMILY, LED BY HIS PASTOR FATHER.
BUT HE HARBOURS A SECRET PASSION FOR
A BLACK METAL GROUP, BRYGHT GEHENNA,
AND BECOMES READY TO EMBRACE DESTRUCTION
AND DARKNESS.

Published in association with the
Museum of Witchcraft and Magic,
these special Rough Trade Editions
seek dialogue with the culture
and folklore of magical practice.
Through hallucinatory fiction,
illustration, a deeply personal essay
and the fates, a range of artists
collaborated to create new works
that take their shape from the
fascinating, alternative history
of the museum.

ROUGH TRADE BOOKS

MUSEUM OF WITCHCRAFT AND MAGIC

9	7	8	-
1	-	9	1
2	7	2	2
-	7	1	6

ISBN 9
£7·99
9 781912 722716
